Direct Mail – 'Probably the most concept in the world'

Contents

Introduction	1
Marketing your Business	3
What is Direct Mail ?	13
Benefits of Direct Mail	23
Objectives of Direct Mail	31
Seven Steps to Heaven	39
The Direct Mail Process	
Step 1: Find The M.A.N.	43
Step 2: Get Personal	49
Step 3: Wrap It Up	67
Step 4: Add a little JNSQ – Je ne sais quoi	71
Step 5: Show them the offer	75
Step 6: Total Control	79
Step 7: Follow It Up!	87
Direct Mail for Business to Business	91
Other Needs To Know	97
Summary	103
Useful Authorities	106
About the authors	108

Introduction

Introduction

Welcome to the Sixty Minute Business Book – on Direct Mail.

We have written this to enable you to get a general overview of direct mail, to consider the key questions, to highlight the main areas for further research and to be able at the end of the book to say:

"Yes I understand broadly what direct mail means and I am in a better position to say whether or not direct mail might suit me".

Furthermore, as with all books in our series we have written it such that you should be able to read it fully in approximately one hour.

Finally, we have sought to introduce some humour and some character to the book and to this end let us introduce you to Porque – the questioner and your conscience!

He has no opinion – he simply asks you to consider. His job is to help you to ask the right questions, consider the options and have an informed decision.

Porque says he's also cute!

Marketing your Business

I want to market my business

In any economy it is vital to let your clients know you exist and to continually inform them of your range of products and services.

Ah a study in the bleeding obvious!

Yes but many organisations (especially smaller players) fail to do this. Marketing seems to be something only the big players do. It seems too complicated and beyond the financial reach of many smaller and medium size enterprises (SMEs). For them it sometimes appears as though they have to open their doors, lie down on the doorstep and wait for death to take them. But through Direct Mail they can take charge of their own destinies.

What can marketing do for your company?

- Helps break through limitations to growth
- Increases sales productivity & reinforces the sales message
- Creates familiarity about your company, your products, your services and your brand
- Enhances customer focus
- Influences people the sales force cannot reach

That's all very well but I can't afford to advertise on TV. I've tried local radio advertising and local newspaper advertising and I've generally been disappointed in the results.

Not surprised that you didn't do well in the newspaper – with a face like yours. Mind you I would have thought you had a good face for radio.

Yes thank you very much for that.

 Well, we'll discuss TV, radio and newspaper advertising later but there are many ways in which you can market your business at little extra cost.

People

Make sure all of your staff are delivering superb service to your clients. That they are courteous, helpful and friendly. This can have an amazingly positive effect on the word of mouth marketing your clients will spread about your business.

If your people are delivering good service to all your clients and customers, these customers may tell others and will almost certainly provide opportunities for repeat business themselves. If however your people are not providing good service your clients and customers will certainly share their bad experiences.

Rest assured all the statistics agree we tell more people about bad service experiences than we do about good service experiences.

Equally it is important that your people are proud of the service they are delivering and are happy to advise their friends, relations and colleagues to do business with you and your company. If your employees are going home badmouthing you and your business this can undermine many of your other marketing efforts.

Product

Ensure your products work properly and do what they promise they will do. Again this will enhance the word of mouth marketing of your business. The old adage 'build a better mousetrap and the world will beat a path to your door' still works. If your product is the very best marketing your business will be easier.

Place

Make sure your place of work (whether or not it is visited by clients) is clean and as pleasant an environment in which to work as possible. This will affect your staff and in turn this will affect the service your clients receive.

But you don't understand. We have very limited space available in our business. It always tends to look a little untidy

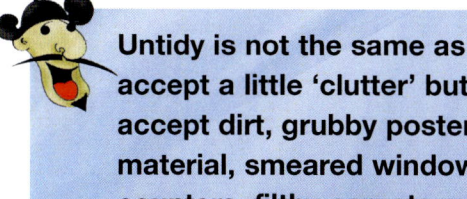

Untidy is not the same as dirty. Clients may accept a little 'clutter' but they will not accept dirt, grubby posters and point of sale material, smeared windows, stained counters, filthy carpets and floor tiles. If you can't take time and trouble to look after your own appearance, how can they expect you to take time and trouble to look after them.

Walt Disney used to have an expression called 'picture perfect' he applied when he was building the first Disneyland theme park.

He was a film maker and used to see the world through a lense. So when he was involved in constructing his theme park he would wander through the park and every now and then he would put the lense to his eye and ask himself 'what's wrong with this picture?'

If there was anything out of place, anything that would undermine the impression he was trying to create he had it changed.

You could try looking at your place of work and asking 'what's wrong with this picture'. If you don't see it your clients certainly will.

Process

Your company processes need to be customer friendly. Occasionally we have processes that seem to exist purely for the convenience of our business, not for the convenience of the client.

Try going into a fast food restaurant at 10.32am and ordering a breakfast which is supposed to finish at 10.30am – bet you won't get your breakfast. You can argue all you want that they have some left over breakfasts they haven't yet sold and it is only two minutes past the time, but policy is policy – even if it is customer unfriendly.

Price

Know your market and decide the appropriate pricing strategy. If you decide to be the cheapest in the market – make sure you are the cheapest. If you decide to price yourself at the higher end of the market, make sure your services, your people and your product can all help to justify this price. Wherever you put yourself on the pricing ladder you need to offer value for money.

**Er... excuse me, I thought we were going to talk about marketing?
We seem to have strayed off the subject a bit.**

**Not at all. It is true that many people only think of marketing in terms of advertising, but marketing is any opportunity when your clients come into contact with your business. Each experience will determine how they view your company, what they say about you to their friends, family and colleagues and, most importantly, whether they start to do business with you and/or continue to do business with you.
Every aspect of your company is a marketing opportunity.**

 OK, I accept that, but can we talk about PROPER marketing.

 OK Jack lets look a the sixth 'P' – Promotion!

 About time too!

Promotion

We briefly mentioned TV, Radio and Newspaper advertising, and all of these channels will help you to reach your clients.

The disadvantage primarily is that these channels can be expensive – see costs.

It is also a blanket marketing approach. It works on the blunderbuss approach – fire loads of shot and you're bound to hit something.

With all these routes you are likely to reach a lot of people who may be interested in your products and that's a good thing, but you are also likely to hit many more people who have no interest whatsoever in your products or services – and you have to pay heavily for the privilege.

More importantly it can be very difficult to identify how much business has been generated directly because of your advertising.

So if TV, Radio and Newspaper advertising is scattered, expensive and difficult to control – what's left?

DIRECT MAIL

What is Direct Mail?

What is Direct Mail?

Establishing one-to-one communication with a targeted group of clients.

'Direct marketing is set to grow at a faster rate than other types of activity, with many companies saying they prefer it to media advertising'

Institute of Practitioners in Advertising

Direct Mail

- Seeks to establish one-to-one communication with a particular group so that recipients perceive they are being addressed personally

- Uses names and addresses sourced from a company's own file or from a rented list in order to mail only those who have purchased or are likely to purchase your products and services

- Directs a mailing piece sent to the target group with the chosen message

- Enables results to be analysed thus revealing how many people responded and whether they bought or would be prepared to buy the product/service in order to ensure that future marketing campaigns can be even more targeted

Direct Mail Quiz

The quiz below is designed to test your perceptions regarding Direct Mail. The answers are on the next page, but don't cheat, have a go – you might be surprised when you compare your perceptions with the answers.

According to the 2003 DMIS Survey

1 How much money was spent on direct mail advertising in 2003?

- a) £10 million
- b) £100 million
- c) £1 billion
- d) Above £2 billion

2 What percentage of consumer Direct Mail is opened?

- a) 12 %
- b) 17%
- c) 68%
- d) 100%

3 What percentage of consumer Direct Mail is read?

- a) 4%
- b) 23%
- c) 40%
- d) 86%

4 How much does the average customer spend through Direct Mail per annum?

- a) £150
- b) £226
- c) £380
- d) £577

5 How much business is generated every year by the Direct Mail industry?

- a) £100 million
- b) £1 billion
- c) £20 billion
- d) More than £25 billion

You will find the answers on the next page along with quite a few other surprising statistics regarding Direct Mail.

Is It Successful?

The DMIS Survey said:

- £2.467 billion spend on direct mail advertising in 2003
- 5,438 million items of Direct Mail sent in 2003
- Volume (+139%) and spend (165%) in last 13 years
- An average of 68% of consumer Direct Mail is opened
- 40% of consumer Direct Mail is read
- Average consumer spends £577 pa through Direct Mail
- Business managers get +/- 14 pieces of direct mail per week
- Managers open 66% or their direct mail
- More than £26 billion worth of business is generated every year by the Direct Mail industry

'It always amazes me that people call Direct Mail 'junk mail' I wish I could have such profitable junk'

What makes Direct Mail different from other forms of marketing?

Targeted

> ' I know half my advertising is wasted –
> trouble is I don't know which half'
>
> *Lord Leverhulme founder of Lever Brothers*

Nobody wants to waste a single penny of their precious marketing budget. One thing is clear, spending time and money to reach people who have no need or money for your product or service is a waste of your marketing spend.

Well I certainly don't want to waste any money. I think we should be clear on that point.

Nobody wants to waste any money.

Well I certainly don't!

I think we got that message.

Targeting is about identifying those clients who have money to spend, or who have an interest in what you have to offer. There's no point in sending a gardening catalogue to someone who lives in a high rise block of flats.

Why Direct Mail?

Targeted

Direct Mail is targeted only to those people who you believe are right for you – so although not everyone will respond as you wish, there is at least a chance that the money and time you spend will reach the people who are most likely to respond.

With Direct Mail you seek:

- To gather information about the individuals you will target.

- Individual data about each target be it the individual's lifestyle, buying history, demographic status etc.

- Not markets, not sectors, not regions but individuals

  With the technology available it is possible to personalise a mailing piece so it is uniquely relevant to the person to whom it is addressed.

- To talk to them individually

  By personalising the mailing piece the target will feel as though they are special and have been considered as a unique individual human being and are more likely to respond as a consequence.

Why Direct Mail?

Cost effective

Because you only spend money reaching your target clients, Direct Mail is more cost-effective.

That's good – I don't want to waste any money.

Measurable

Depending on the response mechanism you incorporate into your marketing programme you can also track, quite accurately, how much business was generated directly as a result of your marketing programme.

Controllable

With a TV, Radio or Newspaper campaign you could reach hundreds of thousands of people. Equally, you pay upfront, for the privilege of reaching so many clients. Imagine introducing a TV campaign and finding that the first TV advert generates enough business for you and your team for the next few weeks.

However, you have paid for TV adverts to run all week. Suddenly you find too much business coming in, more business than you can handle. You find yourself not responding to enquiries – you wish you could turn off your campaign rather than continue to waste money and risk upsetting clients you are not responding to.

With a Direct Mail campaign you control it. You decide how many mailers to send out, your mailing schedule and you can also decide when to stop.

That's good I don't want to waste any money.

Will you shut up.

Benefits of Direct Mail

Benefits of Direct Mail

Acquiring new clients

Direct Mail is a great way of getting your name in front of potential and existing clients and letting them know you exist.

Enhance product/service awareness

Making clients and potential clients aware of your product and service offering is vital to any business. You may use Direct Mail just to inform clients of what it is you and your business can do.

Boost short and long-term sales

Of course we'd also like clients to buy our products and services. You can make sure you design your marketing programme to encourage sales.

Membership renewal

For some organisations the most important thing is to 'tie-in' their clients through 'loyalty programmes' or membership processes.

Direct Mail can be used here to help the organisation to keep in regular contact with their clients/members – informing them of new products/services, getting them to renew their membership, newletters, updates, etc.

Fund-raising

In the days of the national lottery many charities found it imperative to their survival to appeal directly to donors and potential donors. There are a lot of charities clamouring for support. If your charity is to get its due share you will need to make sure everyone knows who you are, where you are, what is your cause, what you want, and most importantly, how they can get their donations to you.

Market research

Sometimes the most important thing is not give your targets information, but to obtain information from them. Sending out questionnaires addressed to individual targets is more likely to gain a response from them.

Build and strengthen the brand

When considering a company's brand we would usually consider the following two areas:

- Brand Awareness
- Brand Value

Direct Mail can help with both of these areas.

Brand Awareness can be increased by ensuring your clients see, hear, touch and feel your name as often as they can. Receiving creative direct mail can be a good way to get your name in front of your clients.

Of course, it is no good getting your name in front of your clients if the message behind your name is not a good one.

Building your brand value (what client's think of when they hear your name) can be strengthened by ensuring your mailing pieces include a pertinent message that is supported by the quality and service offered by your organisation.

One rail company decided to do some TV advertising to promote it's services. The TV advert was shot in black and white through a nice soft filter, and showed lots of smiling porters helping elderly people onto the train. On the train there was plenty of space and the advert showed a grandfather playing chess with his grandson. It was an idyllic scene. Particularly galling for the passengers of that rail company who arrived to travel to work on Monday morning to discover no porters, friendly or otherwise, no space on the train and in many cases no seats available.

This was one example of how marketing can backfire – make sure, before you spend money on your marketing that you can deliver what you promise.

Complement other methods of advertising

If your company can afford to advertise on TV, radio or attend conferences or exhibitions it is vital to maximise the investment through effective follow-up.

Having a direct mail programme that follows up your TV/radio advert can enormously increase the success the campaign.

Running a stand at an exhibition is time-consuming and can be hard work.

It is totally wasted if you spend your time gathering business cards or answering questions from your clients if you are not going to follow-up by directly contacting these clients and potential clients.

Many organisations believe in Direct Mail and it is fast growing it's reputation.

Share of total expenditure in 2002

	2001	2002
Press	50.6%	49.6%
TV	27.3%	25.8%
Direct Mail	12.1%	14.2%
Outdoor & Transport	4.8%	1%
Radio	3.5%	3.3%
Internet	0.9%	1.2%
Cinema	0.8%	1%

Source: World Advertising Research Centre/Royal Mail

After press and TV advertising Direct Mail is the next most popular marketing medium and growing.

'Direct marketing is set to grow at a faster rate than other types of activity, with many companies saying they prefer it to media advertising'

Institute of Practitioners in Advertising

But the internet also seems to be growing. Shouldn't I concentrate on that?

Many people have long claimed that email and websites will lead to a reduction in the use of conventional media. There doesn't appear to be a lot of evidence to support this claim. Inevitably some people will replace mailshots with email, but the majority will more likely continue to use Direct Mail to support and build their on-line presence.

Objectives of Direct Mail

Objectives of Direct Mail

One of the first things you need to decide is what you want your Direct Mail to do for you.

Oh for heaven's sake, there is only one thing Direct Mail can do for me – WIN ME MORE BUSINESS! Even I knew that.

Oh there are many more uses for Direct Mail than just that.

Customer Acquisition

Of course – for many people they want Direct Mail to help them in their customer acquisition.

So let's have a look at the steps involved in a direct mail customer acquisition programme.

What are your objectives?

How many customers?

Before you embark on a direct mail programme you need sit down and identify how many customers you want to contact. It is worth noting that one of the features here will be your awareness of response rates which we will cover in a lot more detail later in this book. But, for example, if we take into account all the variables affecting response rates and we estimate a response rate of 3% - this might give us an idea of how many mailers etc. we need to send out.

Example if we send out 100 mailers, with a 3% response rate we will only attract 3 clients. Is this enough for you?

If you need to attract 100 new clients how many mailers do you need to send out?

Quite honestly I'll be happy with any new business – can't I just do my mailing programme and hope for the best?

Not a good answer Jack – you need to have a plan/an idea at least.

It's all very well hoping for the best now, but as you start committing money time and effort into your marketing programme you may well find your expectations begin to change.

When you only gain 30 clients from sending out 1000 mailers you may be disappointed and surprised simply because you did not prepare yourself for this in advance.

What sales value?

What is your typical order value now?

What is a typical first order value?

If you know the answers to these questions it is worth accepting that the clients you attract with your marketing programme will probably spend more or less the same.

So not only do you need to know how many customers you need to attract you also need to have an idea of what they might spend with you. This will help you when you answer the next question:

How much can I afford?

If you expect your response rate to be only 3% and you send out 100 mailers to attract 3 clients who spend an average of £50.00 with you, you are likely to gain an instant response of £150. If your marketing programme total costs are in excess of this i.e. £300, then you may well be better to try another approach. Of course you should always take into account that the clients you attract may well buy more than once over a period of a number of months/years, that the £150 deficit may be more than covered by these repeat sales.

What is a customer worth?

Do you have any idea of who are the clients you are trying to target?

What do you know about them? Lifestyle, buying history etc.

Is a customer somebody who buys your product or someone who becomes a member or someone who makes an enquiry?

Is it worth it? – Get your sums right

The following checklist is designed to help you calculate how much Direct Mail activity you will have to undertake in order to generate the business you want, and to assess the benefits against the costs.

Let's assume you do everything right and we work on a 3% response rate.

1 What is your budget for your Direct Mail Programme?

2 What is your average order value per customer?

3 What is your cost of sale?

4 What amount of new business will you need to cover the cost of your marketing programme?

For example

Budget	£2000
Average Order Value	£150
Cost Of Sale	30%

Response Rate assumed at 3%

Total Business needed to cover cost or campaign with a cost of sales of 30% = £3000

No. of orders needed to generate £3000 with an average order value of £150 = 20

No of mailers needed to generate a response of 20 orders with a supposed response rate of 3% = 666

Remember this 666 mailers will only cover the cost of the direct mail programme and your cost of sale. This is the minimum level of activity you can afford to do. If you expect to make a profit you will need to at least double this expectation = **1332 mailers**.

Question

Can you afford a Direct Mail programme which consists of 1332 mailers, including design, printing, fulfilment, follow-up and response handling with your budget of £2000?

Of course, you won't need so many mailers if you can either raise your average order value or ensure repeat business from one order.

You need to think this out carefully – after all you don't want to spend £500 on your marketing programme to sell £50 of jelly babies.

Yes that would be a waste of money and I don't want to waste…..

SHUT UP

Sorry.

Seven Steps to Heaven

Well at least to an effective Direct Mail Campaign.

Seven Steps to Heaven

Step One — **Database**

- The foundation of Direct Mail activity and must be
    - up to date
    - validated
    - targeted

Step Two — **Personalise the mailing**

- Creates impact
- Encourages receiver to open
- Says you have taken time to be accurate

Step Three — **Wrap it baby!**

- The Envelope is not just a carrier
- The envelope is packaging!
- Hand written or window – no white labels!!!

Step Four — **Be creative**

- Encourage people to open their mail
- Entice, amuse and tease

Step Five — Only promote a strong proposition

- Everyone has a price
- Look to provide / promote high perceived value
- Give real benefit to the recipient

Step Six — Control!

- Only despatch what you can follow-up
- Calculate the direct response
- Turn the programme on/off – like a tap

Step Seven — Follow up

- The Mailing is only a door opener
- The Mailer will lead to a contact
- Be persistent

The Direct Mail Process

Step 1: Find The M.A.N.

The Direct Mail Process

Step 1: Find The M.A.N

That's a bit sexist isn't it?

No the M.A.N it's an acronym. It stands for the person with the Money, Authority and Need (for your services).

Oh I see. So how do you find this M.A.N then?

You need to profile your client.

Profiling Your Client

The more you know about the clients who are likely to buy from you, the better you can prepare your marketing programme to have maximum appeal to those clients.

Consumer Profile

If your client is an individual consumer i.e. a private homeowner as opposed to a business client here are some of the areas to consider.

- ***Name & Address***

    Having your client's first and second names. Full names are better than initials.

- ***Age & gender***

    Do you have any idea as to the ages and genders of your clients?

    If you are planning to buy a list you may well find many lists will come with client's ages or gender identification. If you know that your best chance of selling your product is to men over the age of 30, you could buy a list which contains information about both age and gender and then send only to those men over 30 on your list.

- **Products, bought or enquired about**

   Do you have any information that tells you what types of products your target clients like to buy?

   What specific products appeal to what specific types of clients?

- **Payment details**

   How do your target clients pay for your products and services?

   Perhaps they only pay by credit card – in which case you could buy a list of credit card holders. If they only pay by cash you might buy a list excluding credit card holders.

- **Recency and frequency**

   If you know how often (**frequency**) your clients typically buy your product and you know that they typically buy from you once every two years, you can also look at when was the last time they bought from you (**recency**). If you know that they typically buy from you every two years and they haven't bought from you for almost two years, then you have a good chance of sending out marketing material that will have an almost immediate appeal.

- *Promotional responses*

Do you have any idea of the kind of marketing campaigns that have received successful responses from your clients?

If your clients are more susceptible to pre-paid response cards, telephone follow-up calls, tear off and send-back coupons, it will give you some idea of the response mechanism to introduce into your marketing programme.

And just how am I supposed to find this information?

**Have you done any previous marketing campaigns? What response mechanisms received the best response? What response mechanism worked less well?
Are you a member of any business network group, Chamber of Commerce, small business federation? Ask your fellow members about the marketing campaigns they have used and the response mechanisms they tried. Are there any lessons here for you? Careful though, they may be in very different businesses from you and therefore the response mechanisms they use might not be appropriate for you.**

The Direct Mail Process
Step 2: Get Personal

The Direct Mail Process

Step 2: Get Personal

The more you know about your potential clients the better.

> Well I know that Mrs Smith has been seeing a lot more of the milkman since Mr Smith went onto nights.

> That's not what I mean. Who on earth cares whether or not Mrs Smith is seeing the milkman?

> Mr Smith does.

> You need to know other things about your clients.

You need to know other things about your clients. Some of the things that will help you with your Direct Mail:

- *Lifestyle*

    You know, for example that people who typically buy your product also often live in detached houses and are often two car families and have incomes of over £35,000 – you could perhaps buy a list of people who fit this particular lifestyle characteristic. There are many lifestyle lists of this kind.

- *Business Profile*

    If your target clients are other businesses you will need to consider other questions, such as:

    - *Name & Address*

        Obviously you want a list of clients' company names and addresses – just as you would with the consumer database

    - *Title or Function*

        Do you have an idea of target job title or job functions?

If you know that your ideal clients are sales directors or people involved in the HR function then you should aim to buy a list with this information.

Slow down. There is a lot more to consider than I thought.

There always is.

Ok, tell me everything I need to know!

I can't tell you the answers, but I can give you a list of the questions to ask.

That will do fine.

Well it depends whether your targets are consumers – end users, or whether you are targeting other businesses.

The questions change depending on who you are targeting.

Consumer Profiling Checklist

1 Age range of clients you are looking to attract?

2 Type of house they are most likely to live in?

3 Type of car they are most likely to drive?

4 Type of job they are most likely to do? (eg. Manual, managerial, administrative etc.)

5 Marital status?

6 Children – yes or no?

7 Educational level? (GCSE's, A levels, University Degree.)

8 Credit Card holders – yes or no?

[   ]

9 Anything else you know about your target client?

[   ]

The more information you know about your target client the easier it will be for you if you decide to buy a list of potential clients to contact.

Business type/SIC code

Are there any particular types of business or specific industries to which your products would appeal?

You can buy lists of clients who are all in a specific industry or who fit a specific SIC code (Standard Industry Classification)

It is, however, well to be aware that, at the time of going to press, the SIC codes are a little out of date. There are many many SIC codes relating to practically every type of Agriculture but only a very small number related to IT-related organisations. You may be better to look for lists of business who fit a specific industry than the SIC codes.

- *Size – employees, turnover, etc.*

    Do you know what size of company in terms of either number of employees or turnover usually buy your products?

    Are they limited companies, PLCs, sole traders or partnerships?

    Again knowing this can help you in terms of buying appropriate lists.

- *Equipment – computers, company cars etc.*

    What types of fleet cars, computer equipment, office equipment, premises, pension arrangements do your target clients typically have?

- *Buying and promotional behaviour*

    What is your target client's typical buying process – do they only buy through purchasing departments or do they always seek three different quotes and always take the middle quote?

    How does your client typically promote themselves? Your client may be more receptive to a promotional channel they themselves use.

Some customers are more easily acquired than others

It is worth keeping in mind that when you embark on a Direct Mail campaign for the first time you may well be tempted to stretch this new marketing medium to the limits.

> Of course I'm going to test it. I want it to help me reach the most difficult clients imaginable.

> Well if you do that don't be surprised if you don't get a great response.

Be reasonable – difficult clients are difficult clients. They are not suddenly going to become incredibly easy just because you send a mailer to them.

If you are new to Direct Mail don't immediately use it to pursue impossible clients.

Your acquisition programme should be based on acquiring the lowest cost sales first

Not low value clients but low cost.

In other words let's figure out which clients are most **LIKELY** to buy from us and market to them. You will find a much higher response to this sort of campaign and a much better return on your investment.

Prospects with similar characteristics might provide a good opportunity to upsell or cross-sell

Try using your existing clients as a database if you believe there are opportunities to upsell or cross-sell to them.

- ***Buy, try, enquire, attend?***

  When putting together your mailing piece you should also give some thought to what it is you hope to achieve with your programme.

  Do you want your client to buy directly as a result of receiving your mailing?

  If so, you will probably have a lower overall response rate than if you only expected them to make an enquiry for more detail.

  Of course you might be inviting them to attend an event – a training course for example, or you might want them to try your product – book clubs for example can work in this way.

  Whichever response you expect will have an impact on your overall rate.

- **Enquiries – loose or tight?**

    If you do want an enquiry is it a loose enquiry 'send me some more details' or is it a tight enquiry 'I'd be happy for a salesperson to call to give me some more details'?

    This too will affect your response rate.

- **Key decision maker?**

    If you have a list or if you are planning to send a mailing piece to people from a list you have bought, have you got the name of the decision maker? - the M.A.N. - the person with the money, authority and need, or is it more likely to land on the desk of an influencer – a teenage child who needs to influence their parents to buy for them, or a gatekeeper, a secretary who has to screen their bosses mail?

    Whichever, it will affect the response rate you are trying to achieve.

The Direct Mail Process

The List

Before you can send a piece of Direct Mail you need to have a list of people to who you will send your piece.

Thank you for that piece of genius advice.

Yes, but there are several important considerations when choosing your list.

The response rate you can expect from your Direct Mail campaign will depend heavily on the quality of the list you choose.

Usually the list will come from one of two sources.

Either your will already have your own database of clients or prospects, or you will buy a list.

Each has their own advantages and special considerations.

Let's look at each one in turn.

Using Your Own List

There are some major advantages to using your own lists.

You and your own team have gathered the list through existing clients or through effective prospecting activity. But you need to ensure the following:

- *Has the information been entered correctly on your database?*

    If information is entered into the wrong field this will have an impact when you mailmerge the data onto your mailing piece, e.g. having both the first name and surname entered into the same field so that the letter starts as 'Dear Geoff Marsh' as opposed to 'Dear Geoff' as you wanted.

- *Has the information been validated?*

    There is no point in sending marketing material to people who have moved jobs, moved house, or who have simply gone away.

The rate at which business data is becoming obsolete is increasing. It grew from 19% in 1998 to 24% in 2002.

Trying to validate your own list can be a massive headache.

It's almost like painting the Forth Bridge. By the time you've finished painting one end it's time to start again at the other. By the time you've finished validating your list there will still be a number of people who have gone away since you started the validation.

No point in trying to validate then?

No you have to validate or you will end up wasting money sending to people who have gone away, changed jobs, moved house etc... And we all know you don't want to waste money.

How did you know that?

You do need to validate your list.

It is good practice to validate only those people to whom you are planning to send your mailing piece.

Buying A List

- *Lists are perishable*

    Just as with your own list, people go away. A list you have bought six months ago is unlikely to be very accurate. If you are going to buy a list you increase your chances of the list being accurate if you use the list you have bought almost immediately.

- *Has the list been well maintained?*

    We know that we have to work hard to maintain our own databases. Has this list come from a reputable source. When was the information gathered? When was it last updated?

- *Mailing history*

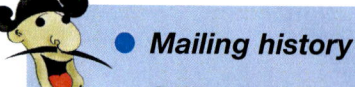

    Some lists are used by a lot of companies. Your success rate is likely to be lower if every company in your industry is using the same list.

    How often has this list been sold?

    Who has been using it?

- *Cost*

    Lists vary in price enormously. Some list brokers will only sell you a list of 1000 names or more. This is not so cost effective if you are only planning to send out 300 mailing pieces.

    A good source of buying names is www.marketingfile.com

    Here you can buy only one name if you wish. You are only charged for the names you use.

    For businesses try Thomson online www.thomsonlocal.com

- *Restrictions* (single use, multiple use, approval of list owner)

  Some lists are for single use only. i.e. you can send just one mailing piece to them. If you wish to send a second mailer you need to pay again.

  Check whether you are buying the right list to send multiple mailers or single use only. You will need to ask the list provider for the answer to this question.

No point worrying about that. If I buy a once only list and just use it over and over again who is going to know?

List providers are not stupid. They will often include a couple of 'seeded' names – fake names where if you mail to those people it will go straight to the list provider and they'll know.

The Direct Mail Process
Step 3: Wrap It Up

The Direct Mail Process

Step 3: Wrap It Up

The Mailing Piece

Now you have decided who you will send your mailing piece to, you need to create it.

When doing so, follow these guidelines:

Attract the Client's Attention

When designing your piece you need to make sure your mailing attracts the client's attention.

- **Powerful headline**

    'Freddy Starr ate my hamster' was an enormous success as a Sun headline. Nobody can really remember the story but everyone remembers the headline. Your headline should aim to grab the attention and increase the chance of the recipient reading your mailing piece.

Visual

Make sure your mailing piece looks unusual – photographs, striking logos, not too much text.

Unusual (sizes & formats)

Be creative. People receive a lot of information today. You need to make sure yours stands out. Look for different sizes, colours, shapes, materials.

Colour

Colour helps recall and persuades people to read.

The Direct Mail Process
Step 4: Add a little JNSQ - Je ne sais quoi

The Direct Mail Process

Step 4: Add a little JNSQ – Je ne sais quoi

Create Interest

- **Answer the headline**

    It's ok to say 'Freddy Starr ate my hamster' but the article below has to explain the headline, and of course it has to be true.

- **Benefits before features**

    It is a good sales technique to make sure that you sell the benefits of your service or product before you start to list and detail the features.

    Remember, people don't buy services for what they do. They buy services for what those services can do for them.

- **Highlight offer**

    Don't hide the services you are promoting. Make sure the offer is clear and easy to find.

- **Short sentences**

    People will not take a lot of time or effort to read what you have written. Keep the sentences short and easy to read.

- **Get to the point**

    Keep it short.

- **Edit, edit, edit**

    Keep it short.

I think it's a good idea to keep it short!

Smart guy!

The Direct Mail Process
Step 5: Show them the offer

The Direct Mail Process

Step 5: Show them the offer

Create Desire

- **Show the product**

    A picture paints a thousand words, as they say. A photograph of your product or service will have a much bigger impact than a paragraph of text.

- **Put the prospect 'in the picture'**

    With today's technology it is possible, using variable data printing to personalise the mailing piece to an individual client. For example, if your mailing piece was designed to sell cat food, you might include a picture of the client's type and colour of cat.

- **Repeat the benefits/offer**

    People remember better when they see or hear something more than once. It is a good idea therefore to repeat the benefits and offer at the beginning and at the end of the piece.

Convince The Reader

- **Appropriate tone of voice**

    Do you want to make a 'jokey' appeal, or take a more formal approach? What voice would work best with your clients?

- **Testimonials**

    Could you include comments and references from some existing users of your products or service?

- **Product specifications**

    Is it appropriate to include details of your products specifications? Will this attract your clients?

- **Strong guarantees**

    Are there guarantees you could include to convince the client of the value of your product?

- **Comparison tables**

    Are there any comparison tables you could use to show your products superiority over other companies or other products?

    (You need to check the legality of this).

Generate Action

- **Tell the reader what to do**

    Make sure that your mailing piece clearly indicates what it is you want the recipient to do Do they need to make a telephone call?, visit a store?, mail back?, or just respond to a follow-up telephone call?

- **Inform of next steps**

    Tell your recipient what the next few steps will be.

- **Closing date**

    State when your offer or competition will come to a close.

- **Easy to reply (Freephone, web site, response mechanism, pre-paid envelope)**

    Make it easy for your clients to respond through mechanisms such as pre-paid envelopes or freephone telephone lines.

If you want to see some examples of good and bad pieces of Direct Mail plus some tools to help you improve your response rate you could visit the Royal Mail web site which gives some valuable insight into this whole area.

The address is: www.royalmail.com/portal/rm/home/

The Direct Mail Process
Step 6: Total Control

The Direct Mail Process

Step 6 – Total Control

Boosting Your Response

If the list is properly validated within the two previous months before your programme commences, it is possible to achieve a much higher response percentage. You need to ask yourself:

- Was the list validated?
- How was the list validated? (e.g. tele-validated)
- Who did it?
- When was it done?

Other things you can do to boost your response:

- ***What's the big idea?***

    Be creative – try to think of an approach no-one in your industry has ever taken before – you can, however, find ideas from other mailing pieces from other industries for inspiration.

- ***Know who you are selling to***

    The more targeted your mailing piece the more successful it is likely to be.

- ***Powerful Offer***

    Try to include an offer too good to resist – discounts, free samples, unique products.

- ***Personalise/customise***

    Mailings with the client's name and references to things in the client's world are more likely to attract his/her attention.

- ***Testimonials***

    Including words of endorsement from reputable and satisfied clients can go a long way to persuading others to follow.

Nobody believes testimonials do they? After all who is going to put in a bad testimonial?

What client is going to give you a good testimonial if they don't mean it? Have you ever been asked for a reference for someone you didn't like? It's almost impossible to just say 'Yes this person is a really great person' if you don't believe it. Even if we weren't concerned about any legal comeback on misrepresenting ourselves and the other person, most of us won't commit to paper a view unless we mean it. Clients and potential clients are often much more affected by testimonials than we think.

Testing

One of the many advantages to Direct Mail is you can 'test' your programme prior to putting it to full use.

You can use testing to discover what works and what doesn't.

What to test:

- ***List***

    Lists can come from many sources, some reputable and some less so. If you are unsure about whether or not you are sourcing your prospects names from the right list you can always try mailing to fifty names from one list and fifty from another. Compare the results. Which list proved better for you?

- ***Offer***

    Which offer will most attract your client's attention? A discount? A free trial? Try mailing to fifty clients with one offer and fifty with another.

- **Timing**

    Is it OK to send out a mailing just before Christmas? Will this get you the results you want? Try mailing fifty just before Christmas and fifty in February. See whether it makes any difference.

- **Format**

    A postcard mailer? A glossy leaflet in an envelope? A Newsletter-type mailer? Which will work best for you? Try fifty of each and see.

- **Creative**

    Which of your many creative ideas will strike home? The triangular or the round envelope? The cardboard pop-up structure in the shape of Elvis or the pop-up in the shape of John Wayne? Try a number of each and see

Testing is not essential. And it is not necessary to test every single aspect of your mailing. These are a few suggestions of what you might test.

Response Rates

The last time I did a direct mail campaign I only managed a measly 2% response rate.

So what?

Thanks for the sympathy.

No, I mean, what did you deduce from the fact that you only got a 2% response rate?

That my programme was a failure, that I'm a failure, that my whole life is a failure, that I should chuck it all in a live in a cardboard box underneath Waterloo Bridge.

Well that's not necessarily true….. perhaps apart from the bit about Waterloo Bridge.

Average Response Rates

There are no guarantees when it comes to response rates.

Even someone who guarantees a 3% response rate to you is probably not telling the truth. You see there are so many variables when it comes to determining response rates.

> **The average response rate to campaigns tracked was 6.5% (excluding all campaigns that received over a 30% response).**
>
> **Overall, response to consumer mailings was slightly better than business-to-business mailings.**

Source: The Direct Mail Information Service – a report entitled Response Rates 2000. A current report can be obtained from their website **www.dmis.co.uk**

The Direct Mail Process
Step 7: Follow It Up!

The Direct Mail Process

Step 7: Follow It Up!

If you really want to increase your success rate then make sure you follow-up. A telephone call is one of the most successful ways of doing this (although you could try an email follow-up or fax follow-up if you wished).

Response rates depend on so many things.

- How effective were you in identifying your target market?
- Was the list validated?
- Was the mailing piece appropriately designed to appeal to your target market?
- Was the offer creative and attractive enough to encourage a response?
- Was your programme well-timed?
- Did you follow-up your mailings? A 1 in 25 response is high for a mailing with no follow-up.

When you say 'response' what do you mean?

- If a response was expected to be a firm order with money sent – don't expect a phenomenally high response rate to one mailer.

- If you determine a response as an enquiry only you are likely to get a higher response.

Measure Sales – Not Response

If your programme is a customer acquisition programme it is much more important to measure sales and actual order value rather than response rate.

If you achieve only a 2% response rate to a mailer for a new car and the order value is upwards of £26,000 and the programme only cost you £1,000, most would argue that is a pretty good return.

If you managed to achieve an 80% response rate of enquiries, but not a single order, most would not consider that a good result.

- How many new customers/members resulted in your mailing programme?

- How much money was generated as a result of your programme both in terms of initial orders and repeat business?

Direct Mail For Business to Business

Direct Mail For Business to Business

Is there really any difference between a business to business market and say a business to consumer or service or retail market?

If so, is there really a difference in the application of direct mail as a marketing tool?

The answer is **YES** and **YES** and to this end I want to spend the next couple of pages just highlighting some of the key aspects of 'B2BDM' and why Direct Mail is particularly suited to a B2B environment.

Firstly let us consider the means one business can get new business from another business!

In truth there are only probably four ways.

1. Advertise/Website

Fairly passive in that you are effectively waiting for a customer/prospect to respond to the ad or information on the web. Not to be dismissed but generally best for creating awarness

2. Mail shot

Sending a mailshot to a database will result in a 1% - 3% response rate - excellent if you have a high value product to sell (luxury car; insurance etc) but of less value for mid range products.

3. Telesales

More personal than a mailshot and if done in conjunction with a mailing will result in better returns.

The issue with all three of the above is that you are essentially engaged in a one dimensional sell.

You are either asking the prospect to respond because your offer intrigues them; or you're offering a more competitive price.

With all three of the above it is very difficult for you to add value, and to be truly successful in selling to another business you need to add value.

*To be able to add value, sell service, promote the range, explain **your** key benefits you **must** get face to face with your prospect/customer.*

4. Face to Face Selling

In a business to business environment **the most effective sales** method is 1-2-1/face to face.

So how do you get 1-2-1?

Again there are proven methodologies.

a) Referrals

Where an existing customer, colleague, friend, family member or even a supplier introduces you to a contact – thus providing you with a 'warm introduction'.

b) Networking

Meeting with people of a similar type with the express objective of discussing business opportunities and/or opening doors for each other with 'colleague businesses' an extension of the adage:

'it's not what you know, but who you know!'

Various business/lunch clubs, Chambers of Commerce, Business Network International etc. exist purely to promote networking.

c) Appointments

Whilst referrals and networking are excellent methods for getting you in front of a new prospect you must not and cannot rely solely on these two approaches.

Getting in front of new prospects by making a business appointment is a proven and effective method of generating new business.

This is where **targeted** direct mail really comes into its own. You use a direct mailing piece to create the awareness and open the door, and follow this up with a positive phone call with the **sole** purpose of simply getting an appointment.

3. Telesales

More personal than a mailshot and if done in conjunction with a mailing will result in better returns.

The issue with all three of the above is that you are essentially engaged in a one dimensional sell.

You are either asking the prospect to respond because your offer intrigues them; or you're offering a more competitive price.

With all three of the above it is very difficult for you to add value, and to be truly successful in selling to another business you need to add value.

*To be able to add value, sell service, promote the range, explain **your** key benefits you **must** get face to face with your prospect/customer.*

4. Face to Face Selling

In a business to business environment **the most effective sales** method is 1-2-1/face to face.

So how do you get 1-2-1?

Again there are proven methodologies.

a) Referrals

Where an existing customer, colleague, friend, family member or even a supplier introduces you to a contact – thus providing you with a 'warm introduction'.

b) Networking

Meeting with people of a similar type with the express objective of discussing business opportunities and/or opening doors for each other with 'colleague businesses' an extension of the adage:

'it's not what you know, but who you know!'

Various business/lunch clubs, Chambers of Commerce, Business Network International etc. exist purely to promote networking.

c) Appointments

Whilst referrals and networking are excellent methods for getting you in front of a new prospect you must not and cannot rely solely on these two approaches.

Getting in front of new prospects by making a business appointment is a proven and effective method of generating new business.

This is where **targeted** direct mail really comes into its own. You use a direct mailing piece to create the awareness and open the door, and follow this up with a positive phone call with the **sole** purpose of simply getting an appointment.

The seven stage process in brief would be

- Select your target companies
- Validate the contact or contacts
- Utilise/check through the telephone preference service
- Send an appropriate mailer
- Follow-up with a phone call after 3/4 days

  ○ ***Three objectives***

  - Make an appointment (primary)
  - Send literature (secondary) good excuse to follow up again later!
  - Get a sale (tertiary)

- Attend the appointment

  ○ Take appropriate collateral

  ○ Always leave something behind

  ○ Never leave without a reason to recontact
- Evaluate/Analyse

NOTE: If you get a 'no' when you follow up don't despair retry for it can take 6-7 'hits' to get an appointment.

Other Need To Knows

Other Need To Knows!

Although we have been highlighting the positive aspects of Direct Mail you need to be aware of legislation that affects whether or not you can send Direct Mail to your clients. In this regard you need to be aware of the provisions of the Data Protection Act.

Data Protection Act

Under the 1998 Act 'data users' become 'data controllers'.

A data controller – person who determines the purpose for which and manner in which any personal data are processed.

Data processor – a person (other than employees of the data controller) who processes the data on behalf of the data controller.

Data controllers are, by law, required to provide an opt-out box. They must be explicit about the right of a data subject to opt out from direct marketing, not only from third parties, but also from the data controller itself.

It is best therefore to give two opt-out boxes on your mailer. One box would allow an opt-out from the data controlling company (in most cases this would be you). The other would give an opt-out from the third party contact.

An example of an opt-out statement:

XYZ Ltd (or via agents) may email, or phone offers reflecting your preferences. Tick if you don't want to receive offers from us ☐ or from third parties ☐.

Further Information:

For a copy of the DMA's book: Guide to the Data Protection Act 1998 – For Direct Marketers, call the DMA on 020 7321 2525 or access **www.dma.org.uk**

Prior to June 2004 this opt out only applied to consumers, sole traders and partnerships. Limited businesses could not opt out. In June 2004, however, the law changed. An individual's ability to opt out of receiving unsolicited telephone calls was extended to include all businesses.

It is an offence to make an unsolicited call to any business that has registered its telephone numbers with the Telephone Preference Service (TPS).

You should not, therefore, make any unsolicited calls to any business without first checking that the company has opted out under the TPS.

Even existing clients, who have registered with the TPS should receive contact call from you unless they have specifically asked you to call.

How to check individual companies to see if they are registered with the TPS?

The most cost-effective method for you to check a small quantity of telephone numbers against the TPS service is to use the Safe2call Premium Rate Service from Operator Services Ltd (OSL).

You will need to:

- Phone 0906 681 0000 (charged at 25p per minute, inclusive of VAT)

- Dial the company telephone number on the keyboard. Continue until you have checked all of your numbers

- Up to three telephone numbers can be checked for TPS listing per minute

- This will be charged directly onto your telephone bill so you pay only when you use the service and don't incur any minimum fee

At the start and end of each call to OSL, a unique reference number will be quoted which you should note down. In case of a query and you need to contact OSL, they will be able to refer to your call and the telephone numbers you have checked with this reference number.

Further information can be gained from Operator Service Ltd (OSL):

Operator Service Ltd (OSL)
The Boat House, 47 Rock Road, Torquay TQ2 5DT
Tel   01803 390080
Fax   01803 390089
e-mail enquiries@osl2000.com
www.osl20000.com

How to check your entire database/mailing lists against TPS

Energetic Enterprises

Energetic Enterprises can screen your entire database against TPS. You will need to:

- Contact Energetic Enterprises and arrange an account or payment. The cost of screening is £1.75 per 1000 names or a minimum charge of £25.00.

- E-mail the company names and telephone numbers in an Excel spreadsheet to: energetic@compuserve.com requesting that your data is screened against the TPS.

- Your data will be screened and returned within 24 hours. If a telephone number has been registered with the TPS, it will be flagged.

Summary

Summary

So that's everything you need to know about Direct Mail.

Yes it's answered all of my questions.

It has?

Yes don't sound too surprised – I'm not thick you know.

I now know what Direct Mail is and how it can help my business and I know the steps and considerations when putting together my Direct Mail programme.

Well good for you.

It is important to remember that Direct Mail is one of the most effective marketing forms for small and medium size businesses as well as large businesses. It does take a lot of work, but at least you know what to do and how to do it. If you follow the steps outlined in this book success should not be too far behind.

Now I'm going off to profile some clients.

You mean you're going to find out about their lifestyles, names and addresses and hobbies and interests?

No I'm going to find out what Mrs Smith is doing with the milkman

I give up...
Goodbye Jack.

Goodbye Porque.

Useful Authorities

Direct Mail is subject to the same laws and codes as other advertising media.

A number of bodies administer these codes and for your reference these are listed below.

Thee British Accreditation Bureau (QMP)

Planwell House
Edington Way
SIDCUP
Kent
DA14 5EG

Tel   0870 606 2001
Fax   0870 607 2001
Email info@qmponline.co.uk
www.qmponline.co.uk

The Advertising Standards Authority

Brook House
2-16 Torrington Place
London
WC1E 7HW

Tel   020 7580 5555
Fax   020 7631 3051
Email enquiries@asa.org.uk
ww.asa.org.uk

Mailing Preference Service

DMA House
70 Margaret Street
London
W1W 8SS

Tel   020 7291 3310
Fax   020 7323 4226
Email dma@dma.org.uk
www.dma.org.uk

The Direct Marketing Association

DMA House
70 Margaret Street
London
W1W 8SS

Tel   020 7291 3300
Fax   020 7323 4165
Email dma@dma.org.uk
www.dma.org.uk

Direct Mail Information Service

5 Carlisle Street
London
W1D 3JX

Tel   020 7494 0483
Fax   020 7494 0455
Email enquiries@dmis.co.uk
www.dmis.co.uk

About the authors

Nigel Toplis

Managing Director, Recognition Express

"The worst decision is not to make one; the best is that kissed by good fortune"

Nigel Toplis joined Recognition Express in January 2003 with a driving ambition to establish the image and recognition marketplace in the UK.

Recognition Express is a successful franchise organisation of 25 years standing, and Europe's largest supplier of corporate recognition products, from signs and name badges to promotional products, employee awards, business gifts and full colour poster printing. Recognition Express was also voted the British Franchise Associations Franchise of the Year in 2003.

Before joining the company, Nigel spent – 9 years with Kall Kwik (latterly as Managing Director). He initiated and drove the merger of the two largest quick print franchises Prontaprint and Kall Kwik to form On Demand Communications Ltd. The merger was the first of its kind in the UK.

Prior to On Demand, Nigel spent 12 years at Allied Domecq firstly in the brewery and restaurant divisions, then at corporate head office. He also spent time at Ladbrokes' telephone services subsidiary as Marketing Director.

The force behind Nigel's successes comes from a desire to be seen as the 'best in his business', whatever that business is, and he believes that hard work and integrity are the foundation stones of success.

Throughout his time in business Nigel has studied and utilised Direct Mail extensively and has a passion for its greater use in creating more effective and more efficient business marketing.

When he has time to unwind, Nigel plays the piano – anything from Tchaikovsky to Elton John – whilst drinking fine wine and smoking a Havana cigar.

Geoff Marsh

A graduate of the University of Loughborough, Geoff started his career as an actor before becoming a presenter in 1986 on the Lloyds Bank's 'customer First' Programme. This was one of the largest series of roadshow workshops in the world and was seen by approximately 70,000 staff.

As a trainer and presenter, Geoff has been involved with conferences, seminars and training programmes for organisations such as Wessex Water, Sun Microsystems, Scottish & Newcastle Breweries, Forte Hotels and Kall Kwik.

Geoff is an international trainer and presenter and frequently works outside the UK for organisations such as Lloyds Bank International Private Banking, BNP Paribas, HSBC, Union Bancaire Privee and Unichem.

He is a visiting lecturer on the Swiss Banking School's prestigious executive MBA programme. He has also worked with the Financial Times on their Wealth Management Academy Series.

In addition Geoff is also much sought after as a presenter and after-dinner speaker. He has his own weekly radio show with Swindon FM. This year he has also launched his first Training Video with Temple Video Productions - Powerful Presentations.

He has been a professional actor on stage, television and even cruise ships.